A CELEBRATION OF THE
DREAM MACHINE

GRAHAM SCOTT'S PHOTO ESSAY ABOUT HARLEY-DAVIDSON

A CELEBRATION OF THE
DREAM MACHINE

GRAHAM SCOTT'S PHOTO ESSAY ABOUT HARLEY-DAVIDSON

GRAHAM SCOTT

Longmeadow Press

First published in 1990 as Harley - Davidson

This 1992 edition is published by
Longmeadow Press
201 High Ridge Road
Stamford, CT 06904

ISBN 0-681-40982-7

Produced by Mandarin Offset
Printed in China.

0987654

Overleaf
Left: The side-valve Model K, produced from just 1952 to 1956, was something of a stop-gap machine. *Right:* The Duo Glide was basically a Hydra Glide with rear swing arm and suspension.

ACKNOWLEDGEMENTS

The publishers would like to thank the following organisations and individuals for their kind permission to reproduce the photographs in this book:

Action-Plus/Richard Francis: 8, 10, 49r, 55(inset), 76t, 78

Kel Edge: 1, 16, 28t, 30-31, 73t, 73b, 76b

The French Picture Library/Barrie Smith: 11, 32-33, 39, 48, 49l, 50, 51, 57(inset)

The Ronald Grant Archive: 36b, 43t

The Octopus Group Ltd./Mike Kerley 14-15, Mike Goss 26

The Kobal Collection: 42-43, 62tl, 65

Norman Hodson/Link House Magazine: 64-65

Motorcycle International: 4, 12

Andrew Morland: 22(inset), 22-23, 52-53, 53(inset), 54t, 56-57, 58(main), 59

Don Morley: 2-3, 6, 7, 9, 13, 13r, 15, 20t, 20b, 28-29, 40(inset), 44, 45t, 45b, 46t, 46-47, 54b, 55, 68, 69, 70b, 71t, 71b, 72tl, 72tr, 72b, 74, 77t, 77b, 79

Rex Features: 31t, 38t, 38b, 40-41, 63tl, 62-63, 64,/Sipa: 34, 35, 43b, 67tl,/Lynn Goldsmith: 62tr,/Richard Young: 67tr

Frank Spooner/Gamma: 37, 60, 61, 66-67, 67br,/Alexis Duclos: 67br

Vidocq Photo Library/Richard Francis: 12(inset), 58(inset), 75

Warr's Harley-Davidson, London: 17, 18, 19, 21t, 21b, 24, 25, 27t, 27b, 63tr, 70t

CONTENTS

INTRODUCTION

If you own a Harley-Davidson you don't just own a motorcycle, you own a solid chunk of American heritage. From the big front tyre to the solid rear fender, the lines of any Harley echo those of Harleys past. Just like the British motorcycle industry, Harley-Davidson stuck with the engineering, the style and the character that had endeared the bikes to generations of riders. Unlike the British bike industry, they survived this decision.

The factory would probably have continued selling iron-barreled Shovelheads to their incredibly loyal following had it not been for the onslaught from the East, an attack that sank the British bikes almost without trace and left the US industry virtually dead in the water. They survived, with the help of government import tarrifs and some fast footwork, just as they had survived near bankruptcy several times in the past. The launch of the new Evolution engine in 1984 brought the company reasonably up to date with a product that would attract riders used to the smoothness, reliability and performance of Japanese bikes. The company succeeded in the difficult balancing act of making a modern bike, but a bike that was still definitely a Harley-Davidson.

It couldn't really be said that they haven't looked back since, because they have done little else. Most of the new models, like the Springer and Heritage, all hark back to the Forties and Fifties for their inspiration, trading on their past with considerable commercial success. While a Honda this year bears no resemblance to a Honda of 40 years ago – and indeed sells because of that very point – a Harley-Davidson of 1990 reminds you deliberately of a Harley from 1950.

A classic design will keep on selling well past its proposed sell-by date. Just look at a Porsche 911, a car the factory has been trying to stop making for years. The 911 is still very much a fashionable car in spite of its relative antiquity. For the moment Harleys and 911s are essential items for those with the cash and the image. While affluent buyers keep the production lines of the 911 running, they equally help keep the Harley-Davidson factories in business. Harleys are 'in' for those with the necessary money, which can easily be £10,000. They are currently a vital accessory in the battle of image, carrying considerably more esteen than a Filofax or a set of Porsche keys.

It would be tempting for Harley-Davidson to expand, get more production lines running and ride the wave. But they won't. Like any company, it has had its ups and downs but, unlike some, it hasn't forgotten them. They may be losing potential sales now, but they know that if or when the current craze for their products exhausts itself they will still be there, still selling bikes.

And they will still be there because of a loyal following for whom a Harley-Davidson is the finest expression of the motorcycle experience. Whether they are 60-year-old crewcut rednecks or long-haired rebels half that age, for all of them a Harley is the only real motorbike left in production. You can see and feel things working and moving on a Harley, in a way that you cannot on a fully faired Honda or Yamaha. When you ride one there is a rapport, a physical and mental connection with the machine that extends beyond your backside in the saddle, your hands on the bars and your feet on the pegs. Riding a Harley is not like riding any other bike.

For now this hardcore has to share the experience with the city boys, the Yuppies, the Born Again Bikers and the Rich Urban Bikers, even though they hate being associated with such high-profile groups. But when those groups move on the loyal buyers will carry on stubbornly owning their Harleys, caring for them, customising them, restoring them, riding them. For a Harley-Davidson is not just a motorcycle, it is a way of life.

Left: The sturdy 61 cu in (1000 cc) V-twin launched in 1909 and lasted, virtually unchanged for 12 years. *Right:* The excellent 1982 FXRS, with rubber mounted engine, was about as good as you could get before the 1984 Evolution series.

TOURING

THE ROAD IS LONG AND HOT, SHIMMERING IN THE HAZE OF HEAT COMING OFF THE TARMAC. IN THE DISTANCE

SOMETHING DARK FLICKERS AND WAVERS LIKE A BLACK FLAME, SOUNDLESS. IT GETS LARGER, CLOSER, TAKES

SHAPE AS A FAINT THUNDER STARTLES THE JACK RABBITS. SOON IT IS A BIKE, WITH RIDER AND PASSENGER

WATCHING THE ROAD, THE SKY AND THE SCENERY. THE THUNDER BECOMES A LOUDER RUMBLE AND IS UPON

YOU AND THEN GONE, THE SOUND FADING AS SILENCE RETURNS. A HARLEY IN ITS ELEMENT: RIDE AND SEE ■

Left: Harley-Davidson is No 1. A Sportster in front of typically distinctive H-D advertising. *Above:* The hog on the road — Harleys were born for touring the thousands of miles of freeways in the U.S.

If you want to go a long, long distance on your cycle you have to consider what you need: comfort, plenty of room for luggage and good fuel consumption. You also need a whole lot of torque so you don't have to keep changing gear, and a lazy-feeling engine that doesn't tire you with its frenetic fizz. You need a Harley.

America is as big as the great outdoors and for a big place you need a big bike, capable of rumbling you from state to state with the minimum of fatigue. With a lot of straight roads and a tedious speed limit, ultimate performance and razor-sharp handling are not at a premium, so the Japanese sports bikes that wiped out the English bikes can't get such a grip. Equally, the Japanese now have their own luxury liners, like the GL1200 and 1500cc Aspencades, Yamaha FJ1200s and Kawasaki GTRs, as do the Europeans, with the Moto Guzzi and BMW twins. Harley doesn't exactly have the market to itself, but none of the opposition can match the gentle thunder of a Harley on the road. To an American, freedom is not an impossible dream, it is a God-given right, it is built into the Constitution, and it is symbolized by an American product: Harley-Davidson.

As numerous T-shirts remind you, God rides a Harley, but sometimes He needs a little help. Any patriotic American, or image-conscious European for that matter, would buy a Harley as a matter of course even though there have been times when the product fell below expectations in terms of reliability and performance. However, the Japanese have long had their sights on the lucrative internal American touring market. It is ironic to think that it was Harley-Davidson itself that started the Japanese on this particular road.

Back in the 1930s, when times were hard, H-D managed to generate some income by selling blueprints of current models to a Japanese business consortium. The money helped Harley keep going but it also gave the Japanese an entry into the bike market, helped by subsequent sales to them of tools and machines for bike manufacture from the H-D factory. Ever since, H-D and the AMA (American Motorcycle Association) have been fighting to keep others from not just dominating the market but actually wiping out the company. Charges of dumping brought against the Big Four Japanese firms in the late 1970s didn't really get anywhere, even though the charges proved well founded. Five years later, in 1983, H-D had but five per cent of the US retail market and was heading for the floor. At the last minute some intensive lobbying brought in fairly hefty American import tariffs that hit foreign bikes

Although everyone thinks of touring Harleys as being as big as the road, lots of riders go to rallies and on rides on something much leaner. *Above:* A hog keeps the rider in the wind as he beats his way to Daytona. The helmet on the back means this guy is an optimist. *Right:* The other end of the scale is a fully dressed 1200cc Electra Glide with custom paint and a seriously comfortable saddle.

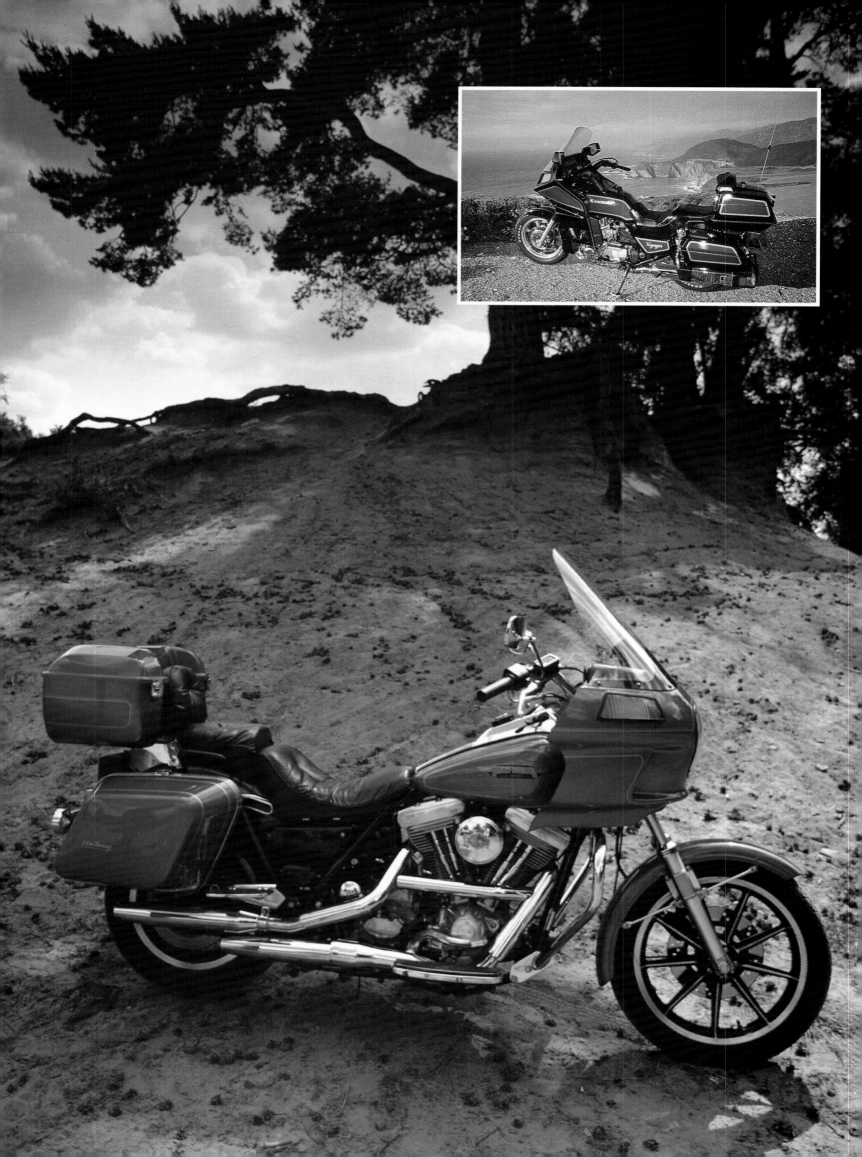

Left: Little and large: the Kawasaki Voyager (inset) makes an Electra Glide look demure and understated by comparison. Although its six-cylinder engine gives a level of smoothness and speed well above any touring or sporting Harley, not everyone wants such a tinsel palace, many preferring the lines of the FXRT (main pic). The fairing of the FXRT was wind-tunnel tested and offers good weather protection – useful for European riders for keeping the rain off, and for American riders for keeping the bugs out of their teeth. Panniers and top box give ample luggage space for most couples on vacation. *Above left:* Lean and long, this Harley in Death Valley shows the influence of the movie *Easy Rider* with bedroll, bandana, denim-over-leather and rear cissy bar. It can be hot and lonely on the road. *Above right:* Not much speed, not many revs, keep it rolling, cruising from dawn to dusk with some beers at the end of a long day.

over 700cc – in other words, bikes in the same league as Harley-Davidson.

The Japanese have responded by trying to shift production away from Japan, with the result that the mile-eating Honda Gold Wing, for example, is now made in America. The other prong of the assault has been the production of big oriental V-twins that mimic H-Ds. Bikes like the Kawasaki Vulcan, a 1500cc V-twin, deliberately ape the torque and looks of a Harley, but there are two main differences: they are invariably cheaper than the real thing – and that is the second difference: they are not the real thing. You can duplicate, mimic, replicate, fake anything from a Rolex watch made in Mexico to a kit-car Lamborghini Countach, but they remain imitations, however well made they are. Nobody else but Harley-Davidson can build a Harley-Davidson, as some of the tinsel toys, the 'Hardly-Davidsons' from Japan graphically display.

The Harley is a uniquely American product, designed by and for Americans. While Europeans can pose around London or Rome on their Sportsters, the bulk of Harleys thunder remorselessly across the American open spaces. The Japanese can design sports bikes and sports tourers for other cultures as well as their own but nobody but the Americans have yet made a bike that so perfectly suits the sheer size of the American land mass. Perhaps it is because Japanese thinking is influenced by a country that is so overcrowded it doesn't even have room for many proper golf courses.

Bikes like the Electra Glide and FXRT were not designed for taking the girlfriend out for a pizza, they were designed to take two people and their luggage from state to state without fatigue. The bikers and the tourers have usually been two separate groups in America, obviously not wanting the same thing in their bikes. The tourers are not always die-hard bikers, they just like loading up their bike and heading off for the weekend or on vacation. The Harley Owners Group (HOG) has more than 100,000 members in the States, who spend a lot of time riding to

rallies and shows, or on charity runs like toy runs. Bikes like the Electra Glide and Tour Glide are easy to ride, letting you get on and enjoy the air, the scenery and the experience of being on the road. You don't have to be young with flexible knees and elbows and hair-spring reflexes to ride them, so owners tend to just keep on owning Harleys, sometimes the same one for decades or else a new one when they feel like it.

Increasing age is looked on in a completely different way in America than it is in Europe. In the States a lot of Harley buyers are in their 50s or 60s and are determined to have a good time. These often born-again bikers may prefer to ride and then check into a motel rather than crawl into a tent, but they ride just the same. They often prefer the dressers, the big Glides with all the extras and, as a group, are not renowned for their left-wing tendencies. Most HOG groups have their fair share of red necks, crew

cuts and political opinions as tolerant as those of Emperor Ming the Merciless of Mong. Turn up to a HOG meeting on an East German MZ at your peril.

Rallies are all part of the lifestyle, with annual meetings in places like Wendover, Daytona and Sturgis – the last has been running since the 1930s and even has a Harley named after it. Charity runs give some purpose to a ride, so the riders can not only enjoy the journey, they can also feel good inside about it. For example, the factory's 85th birthday run in 1988 was called the Milwaukee Ride for Muscular Dystrophy. This was the biggest organized ride in history, raising over $500,000 for the charity. If you are going to ride you may as well feel that you are doing some good for somebody. On the way to a rally or out on a run with a club, you are bound to see lines of bikes, sometimes two abreast, throbbing away the miles, two up, mountains of luggage, shades, black leathers and beards

Left: The Los Angeles Police Department (LAPD) has been running Harleys since the 1930s. This FLH, with a rather shabby and unusual silencer, can park wherever it likes, damn the signs. *Above:* Police Electra Glide gets back on the move after a bust. Note the sheer width and bulk of the front end, and the incredible mirror-finish on the officer's boots. (Well, it's either polish or oil.)

that are as often grey as black.

Such groups seldom break the law out on the road – or at their destination for that matter – but not unnaturally they tend to draw the attention not just of the public but of the police as well. Working on the 'If you can't beat 'em join 'em' philosophy, US police forces have been on Harleys ever since 1909, when Pittsburgh's first motorized vehicle happened to be a Harley. Less than 20 years later, mirroring the factory's incredible growth, more than 2,500 police units were using the big V-twins. Throughout the wars that followed, the Second World War, Korea and Vietnam, sales of H-Ds to the police kept up, with highway patrols proving good customers and the factory, in turn, providing a good service and back up.

However, in the 1970s the factory started to lose their grip, with most police forces switching to four-cylinder Kawasakis. Even the celebrated CHiPs, the California

Highway Patrol, who had been running Harleys since 1930, had a crisis of confidence and switched over. Kawasaki had the price, the speed and the reliability. But slowly, as the Harleys improved and the police forces found that the re-sale value of the Japanese bikes was poor, the American factory started to claw back its traditional market. Now most, including California, have gone back to Harley FXRP Pursuit Glides and FLHT-P Electra Glides. A poster of the time asked the salient question: 'Should your police department's public image be riding on foreign motorcycles?'

Now it is something of a mixture, with police on Kawasakis, and old and new Harley-Davidsons. You can't fail to spot a patrolman on his hog: white bike, red and blue lights, black uniform with knife-edge creases, mirror-shine boots and the inevitable shades. He's on a Harley, on the case and he's cool.

CHAPTER

BEGINNINGS

WHEN YOU RIDE A HARLEY-DAVIDSON YOU ARE RIDING A HERITAGE THAT GOES BACK ALMOST TO THE BEGIN-

NING OF THE CENTURY. SOME MIGHT SAY THAT THE TECHNOLOGY LEVEL OF THE EARLY BIKES IS TOO READILY

APPARENT IN THE LATEST V-TWIN, BUT FOR OTHERS THE SENSE OF HISTORY AND UNBROKEN TRADITION IS

WHAT MAKES THEM WORTH OWNING. NOT EVERYONE WANTS A CARTILAGE-POPPING JAPANESE SPORTS BIKE,

INSTEAD THEY WANT A BIKE WHICH HASN'T CHANGED IN SPIRIT FOR AT LEAST 80 YEARS, IN A WORLD THAT

CHANGES TOO RAPIDLY FOR COMFORT ■

Left: The Milwaukee factory at Juneau Avenue, still flying the flag. *Above:* Taken in 1916, this photo shows survivors of the First World War going for a recuperative ride on early Harleys. Two years later Harley-Davidson was the biggest-selling bike manufacturer in the world.

In the 1890s the French Count Albert de Dion formed a socially unlikely alliance with the artisan Georges Bouton. Their common interest was the new petrol engine principle, derided by Bouton's former partner: 'How can a motor function on a series of explosions?' he demanded. But by the turn of the century the engine was working efficiently, if not putting out much power. The principles embodied by it made their way across the Atlantic and engines based on the de Dion single cylinder soon began to appear. Indian were the first, in 1901, followed by others such as Mitchell, Merkel and Yale. Then in 1903 three men in Milwaukee produced a single machine that was sturdy, reliable and good looking: Bill Harley and Arthur and Walter Davidson had, if not arrived, at least come over the horizon.

Art Davidson drew up the basic plans, Bill Harley designed the bike and Walter actually made it. And somebody bought it: the first link had been forged in a commercial chain that stretches to the present day. Following the sound principle of 'Don't give up your day job yet' they worked on their hobby only in their spare time, so by 1905 they had only made 11 bikes in total. But by 1907 this had increased to 150 and they had themselves a company, an employee and works premises – a wooden shed built for them by the Davidsons' father.

The single cylinder bike improved, with input from a neighbour, Ole Evinrude, who was on his way to fame with his marine engines. Even though Bill Harley left to study for an automotive engineering degree, with the help of another Davidson, eldest brother William A., the company started to expand at a rapid rate, soon employing nearly 20 people in a purpose-built brick factory. It all seems surprisingly simple, following the American ethos of hard work and innovation.

Above: Three modes of transport, all dedicated to getting the mail through. This 1911 35 cu in single-cylinder proved more useful than a horse and cart in getting mail to rural areas. *Right:* The first president of Harley-Davidson, Walter Davidson, photographed in 1908 beside the bike on which he had just won the Long Island Endurance Race – the machine is very similar to the first 1903 model except for sprung leading-link forks.

Top: Beautifully restored First World War vintage single, a 5-35, which stood for 5 bhp and 35 cu in. Note that belt drive has gone over to chain drive, while the rider now had the comfort of a 'Ful-Floteing' saddle. By 1915 the singles had three-speed transmissions, giving a top speed of around 60 mph, with at least some suspension travel – around 2 in from the front leading-link forks. *Bottom:* A 1914 61 cu in (1000 cc) V-twin. The first 61 cu in V-twin was launched in 1909 and remained basically unchanged until 1921. This restored model features chain-drive, a hand-operated oil pump (replacing a gravity-feed system) and a patented idling system.

In 1909 Bill Harley popped over from his studies and ran off the first V-twin by basically grafting a second cylinder on to the first, an innovation soon followed by a rear-hub clutch, step-starter and two- and then three-speed transmissions. This first twin was a V of 45 degrees with a 61 cu in (1,000cc) capacity, two dimensions that have stayed with H-D for a long, long time. The other founders got on with producing the bikes, learning on the way such arts as welding, advertising and accounting. The tempo of the company picked up the whole time until by 1918, when orders were helped by the military, Harley-Davidson was the world's largest motorcycle company. Not bad at all for 15 years work from scratch.

Everything seemed to come their way, with a bit of luck and judgement. When prohibition forced some of Milwaukee's breweries to close, a local motorcycle company was ready to take over their facilities for storage and manufacture. Even the Depression failed to hit hard, at least for a while, but then, as the 1930s progressed, it became clear that motorcycles were going out of favour to be replaced by cars, now being produced at a relatively attractive price. H-D responded by trying any engineering venture they could lay their hands on, like producing parts, sidecars, and even aero engines, but they also refined their product range. This is not to say that, to the casual observer, there was much to make you jump with excitement – for virtually the entire inter-war period H-Ds were based on olive drab colour schemes.

Top: Sales hype for the 74 cu in 1935 V-twins. The side valve 74 cu in bikes were launched in 1930 and proved not reliable ponies but unreliable dogs. By the mid 1930s the factory had improved the product. *Above:* A youthful Fred Warr, the earliest Harley dealer in Europe, aboard an absolute Lulu, a 1925 JE.

1939 39-EL, a sporty and handsome beast of 61 cu in with overhead valves and Special Sport specification. The Knucklehead, so called because of the 'knuckles' on top of the cylinder heads, overcame lubrication problems at its launch in 1936 to become one of the stock and sturdy Harleys.

Above: From left to right: Arthur and Walter Davidson, William S Harley and William A Davidson watch as the first 1936 61 cu in model comes off the line. *Right:* A group of menacing motorcycle scouts pose on their WLA 45 cu in V-twins in 1940. The lack of magazines in the sub-machine guns is a give away – the photo is shot not at the front, but at Camp Gordon in Georgia, USA. H-D produced 90,000 WLAs and WLCs (the latter for Canada) during the war, and built a further 30,000 as spares. These much-loved workshorses won the factory the coveted E-Award for excellence.

But beneath that drab exterior things were going on, such as in-line flat-twins, twin cams, overhead valve singles and the excellent 61 and 74 cu in (1200cc) twins that were derived from board-track racers. But while most other companies in America and Europe tried out all manner of configurations including V-fours and flat fours, H-D came back to the singles and V-twins to the exclusion of all else. However, to produce anything at all in this period was good going, since Henry Ford had sent most bike manufacturers to the scrap-heap. Only Harley-Davidson, Indian, Henderson and Excelsior survived the four-wheeled assault, and by the mid 1930s only Harley-Davidson and Indian were left.

But in 1936 the company was only surviving, it was producing the Knucklehead, the first overhead-valve V-twin, with the valves operated by pushrods. H-D also launched its first four-speed gearbox that year. By 1941 they had progressed to a 74 cu in (1200cc) Knucklehead, now seen as one of the definitive Harleys, but further innovation was curtailed by the war that engulfed the world.

The Second World War caused its own dreadful prob-

lems, but also created a ready market for bikes for armoured divisions, despatch riders, and for Steve McQueen to jump over barbed wire on. During the 1930s the 45 cu in (737cc) twins had been looking prettier and prettier with highly stylized tanks and paintwork, but for the war this model turned into a faithful workhorse, back in olive drab. The WLA 45 cu in was one of the symbols of the American industrial effort, like the Jeep, and did the long-term reputation of the company a power of good. By the time the war ended Harley-Davidson was up and running, but their product range of the 45, 61 and 74 cu in was the same as it had been before the war. Indian was still with them, but a disastrous series of singles damaged the marque beyond repair and the company folded slowly in the 1950s. Not so Harley-Davidson.

In 1948 they started to shake off the war, and came up with hydraulic valve lifters fitted to Panheads. The next year they replaced the springer front end with telescopic forks on a 61 cu in Panhead now called a Hydraglide.

H-D survived another bad spell in the 1950s and decided that they needed a smaller model, possibly a middle-

weight, in their range. Unlike Indian, they decided to go and get somebody else's instead of making their own, and consequently bought half the Italian Aermacchi bike division in 1960. The result wasn't totally happy, although the plant in Varese, Italy, carried on production until 1978. The range of single-cylinder two-strokes made there never sold in large numbers and probably caused some confusion over marque identity since a 125cc two-stroke dirt bike hardly added macho kudos to the Harley-Davidson name. On the other hand, Italian-built Aermacchis – technically Harley-Davidsons – won 250 and 350cc World Championships in the 1970s, so some success came of it. Even more success has come the company's way since it was sold by H-D: it is now known as Cagiva.

Back in the big boy's world came the introduction in 1957 of the Sportster, an overhead valve thunderer, one of the seminal Harleys. Alongside these XL hogs the FL tourers continued to take a lot of people a lot of miles, adding weight, accessories and capacity with the years until the FL finally became the Electra Glide in 1965, adding the aluminium-based Shovelhead motors the following year. However, the Electra Glide, while proving a

Left: The first Hydra Glide, with hydraulic front forks, copes well with the studio floor in 1949. *Above:* 1962 bike show demonstrates the total confusion on the Harley-Davidson – or is at Aermacchi? – stand. Significantly, among all the re-badged Aermacchi singles, the only bike with just 'Harley-Davidson' on the tank is the big Duo-glide at the far right – a 'proper' Harley-Davidson.

27

popular and reliable bike, came at a time of real crisis for Harley-Davidson. Constant and high inflation as well as static profits in real terms meant that the company was increasingly under-financed. Accordingly, in 1965 Harley-Davidson went public, raising necessary cash to re-fund and carry on with development programmes. But that was not the end of the troubles.

By 1968 the company was virtually standing still, trying hard to fend off the oriental onslaught which threatened to wipe them out. A highly conservative management and market in America meant that the company was in no fit state to fend off the technological assault aimed at them from Japan. Harley-Davidson was ripe for acquisition by a predator company, and some of the sharks spotted circling the company would definitely have chewed it up and spat it out, having swallowed all the tasty bits. Accordingly, the H-D management, bearing in mind that a lot of them were Davidsons by now, recommended that the company be sold to AMF, the American Machine and Foundry Company, with interests in industry, yachts and leisure products like bicycles. By 1969 the deed was done and AMF took control, leaving most of the management in place – for the time being.

Under the chairmanship of Rodney C. Gott, AMF poured millions of dollars into the ailing company and also brought in a whole pack of experts – not surprisingly there was instant conflict with H-D's more conservative and traditional management. The first decade of AMF ownership saw about half a dozen presidents come and go. The effect of the acquisition on the products, however, was not nearly as divisive, although bikes produced during the AMF years have the worst reputation for reliability and build quality.

The first AMF bike was the brainchild of Willie G. Davidson, who had seen the trend towards riders trying to improve the FL's front end to make it more sporty by fitting all sorts of after-market forks. The factory response was the 1971 Super Glide, which mated FL and XL parts to make the first FX. This opened the door to a proliferation of models that used the best of both series. Another notable bike was the '77 XLCR Cafe Racer, a breathtakingly beautiful beast that took on the Japanese sports bike stylists head on, even if its specification fell well below the opposition. But all this was largely preaching to the converted, a dependable and totally loyal group of riders. If Harley was ever to make significant inroads into the major market share dominated by the Japanese they had to make a more modern bike, something almost less Harley-Davidson without losing the essential spirit of the machine.

The 1981 Tour Glide was a start, since its rubber-mounted engine cut down on the vibration that put off so many potential riders. When the bike received the new Evolution engine Harley had a bike smooth enough to entice buyers used to the smooth if buzzy Japanese bikes. But the new engine was more than just a smoother unit; it was the start of a new age for the factory.

The species evolved in 1984 with the release of the Evolution engine that was almost totally new although, of

The old and the new. Inset shows cylinder heads at the Milwaukee factory in 1989, while the main photo shows a previous chapter: an Electra Glide from 1976, produced under the ownership of AMF. Note the stereo radio in the fairing, while extra chrome and gold add to the factory taste for slab 'n' chrome.

course, it kept to 45 degrees between its cylinders. The alloy cylinders featured lighter weight, improved combustion, cooler running, a computer-designed camshaft, improved electronic ignition and internal oil lines, although the pistons were made by Mahle and it used a Japanese Keihin carburettor. Top end overhauls, thanks to build quality and the hydraulic tappets Harley designed back in 1948, were claimed to be at 50,000 mile intervals. Gone were the oil leaks, some of the vibration, the over-heating and some of the mechanical noise. In came a smoother, more reliable ride that did wonders for the number of warranty claims, which fell considerably. The revolution was late but it brought Harley-Davidson into the late 20th century at a stroke.

And the revolution came about not under the corporate hand of AMF but at the hands of individuals, lovers of the marque who had bought the company back. AMF had become increasingly disillusioned with the bike market, which took a lot of investment but gave back a small profit to the corporate coffers. Led by Vaughn Beals and Willie G. Davidson, a consortium mostly comprising AMF executives who had faith in the Harley-Davidson name bought back the company and rode back to Milwaukee in a symbolic procession in June 1981 to start on the next stage of the story. Even though Harley-Davidson would almost certainly be smaller and less successful had it not been for the AMF years, since then things have gone from better to best.

In 1986 the company decided to go public, to re-finance and pay off some of the debts. This was a roaring success, with the two million shares heavily over-subscribed by a public keen to get a slice of a rejuvenated company that flew the American flag.

The Evolution range of engines has been one of the major building blocks in the company's success, with the 1986 883 Evolution Sportster selling at first for $4,000, a perfect entry vehicle with a keen price. Furthermore, if you had it serviced by a recognized dealer and then traded it in for a big twin, they would give you the same money back as part-exchange. Five years later the same bike costs just over £4,000 in the UK, a thousand pounds less than it cost back in the pre-Evolution 1980s. In some ways it is still quite a crude machine, built to a price, but if you want a Harley it is more of a bargain now than it has ever been.

The other major success story has been the harking back to the past while keeping a weather eye on the future. The 1984 launch of the Softail, with its apparently solid rear end which actually hides a suspension system, has proved to be one of the prime sellers. Its development into the Softail Heritage and Heritage Classic shows just how well the factory has gauged the public's taste for something old but something new.

All of these factors have combined to pull the company

The modern image: 1940's influence, 1990's prices. The Warr Harley dealership in Chelsea, London, risks a Heritage Softail Classic on the carpet as a centrepiece for all the paraphernalia tucked away in the cabinets.

back from the very brink of extinction. So confident is the factory in its future that it has had the import tariffs dropped, claiming that now competition is a valuable stimulus. Elsewhere in the world sales are buoyant but in America H-D now has an incredible 62 per cent of the market in bikes over 850cc. But although sales have never been better, there are no plans for huge expansion and new manufacturing plants. Harley-Davidson has had its ups and downs before and is taking a cautious view of the current surge in popularity. That might be bad news for those who don't want to wait for their new bike – indeed, it is

certainly costing the company sales – but it is good news for those who would like to see Harley-Davidson living to a ripe old age.

With the company now under the chairmanship of Vaughn Beals with James Paterson as Chief Executive of

the motorcycle division, the future holds the possibility of a new racing engine to match the Japanese and, more certainly, a new 1500cc engine. The new model for 1990, with solid wheels and shotgun pipes, shows the company is confident of its taste and direction - who else but Harley-Davidson would have the nerve to call a bike 'Fat Boy'?

Tourer cum cruiser, a Heritage Softail Classic gleams in the evening light. The tassels, leather and chrome are all standard.

3

REBELLION

FROM *THE WILD ONE* TO *EASY RIDER,* FROM MILWAUKEE TO MUNICH TO MELBOURNE, FROM TEENAGER TO

BORN-AGAIN-HIKER, FROM HELLS ANGEL TO DREAMER, FROM HOLLISTER TO DAYTONA: TO ALL THESE

RIDING A HARLEY IS THE MOVEMENT OF REBELLION. LONG HAIR, BLACK BEARDS, STAINED DENIMS, SHADES,

OIL-BLACKENED FINGERS, RED-RIMMED EYES, BEER, OL' LADIES, BANDANAS, PATCHES, HARLEY'S

BEST, FUCK THE REST ■

If you fancy being a bad-ass Harley bro', some facial hair is essential. The genuine article from the good ol' USA (left) clearly has the edge here on his European counterpart (above). You just can't fake it.

At the end of the Second World War there were a lot of young men roaming America who had been used to combat, excitement and danger – a lot of them had got used to Harley-Davidson WLAs as well. Normal working life, with wife, children and a sensible sedan, didn't seem too exciting after hunting Tiger tanks in France in a Sherman. There had to be another life. Disenchanted men began to join together in loose groups, to go out drinking, riding bikes and generally raising conservatives' blood pressure. There began to be something of a them-and-us mentality, not only between these hard-charging groups and the normal citizen, but also with the straight touring riders, who didn't approve of ripping down main streets with a gut-full of whisky and beer. Besides, these yahoos seemed to attract the prettiest girls.

The atmosphere gradually became charged, until a group of bikers called The Booze Fighters, deeply sensitive, creative souls to a man, rode into Hollister, California, on 4 July 1947 to watch some bike racing. The local citizens became so incensed with their rowdy behaviour that it was only a matter of time before the verbal became physical. The end result was the bike group fighting anyone in town, ripping the place up but only, they claimed, to defend themselves. They felt got at by everyone else, and everyone else felt threatened by them. It made a great plot for a film, with plenty of menace, action and social comment. In 1953 the film based on those events came out and caused a reappraisal of attitudes towards bikers. *The Wild One* featured a young, sneering Marlon Brando, at the head of a threatening, looming pack of

Above: Tattoo artists at Daytona get rich simply because their clients have so much flesh to cover. The Harley-Davidson lifestyle really gets under your skin.

Above and right: A young Marlon Brando in days before he started eating rolls of toilet paper before he spoke. Scenes from *The Wild One* only show one Harley despite their name being linked with the rebels. Note the Matchless 'M' upside down on one tank, and the Triumph Speed Twin (opposite).

True or false? *Above:* Grubby bike and riders, mean looks and straggly beards denote Hells Angels. But, despite the Harley tank, this is a Kawasaki and this is a motorcycle club, not the real thing. *Below:* The patch proudly displays the Angels' colours. The wooden mallet is not an official Harley accessory but comes in useful if the chapter suddenly decides it has to camp for the night, for example. Let's hope he remembers to move it before leaping back on his hog. *Right:* Stars 'n' Stripes and custom chromed air filter are typical 1970s chic.

outlaw bikers, who really were members of outlaw bike gangs. The new image was born, and with that tough image went the name of Harley-Davidson. Although the film went straight for the public's jugular, passing through to take up residence in the national consciousness, few seemed to notice that in the film Brando actually rode a Triumph Speed Twin.

Harley-Davidson, the AMA and the touring and straight riders immediately started trying to project a better image of bikers by going on charity runs, keeping to the letter of the law and having their bikes blessed. Other, more positive biking films came out at the time, but 'nasty' proved to be a more lasting media image than 'nice'. After all, excess is always so damn attractive; sex and drugs and rock 'n' roll were here to stay.

The events at Hollister were photographed by a *Life* photographer, and the drunken, sweaty, beer bellied belligerents staring at the reader set the stage for the next generation of bikers, who went more and more often to the edge of the law and then further and further beyond it – rebels without a pause. Sociologists and Hunter S. Thompson descended on a swelling mass of clubs and

Above: Daytona spring sunshine brings out the mellow in everyone as two bros rap on Main Street. Note the difference in size between Sportster's slim forks (left) and the 80 cu in FL tree trunks (right). *Opposite:* A less happy occasion as Hells Angels form up to ride to friend's funeral. Just about every make of bike from every country is represented. The traditional black is at least appropriate.

gangs that slowly began to get organized: the Outlaws, the Hells Angels. They were the recipient of a certain amount of radical chic, but eventually their actions started to live up to the highly imaginative editorials and rumours, with fights, races at night, heavy drinking sessions, sex with under-age girls and other illegal but fun-sounding pursuits that must have made the conservative, crew-cut touring rider break out in a sweat just thinking about them.

It was all terribly exciting to have some outlaw gang come cruising into town on their huge, rumbling Harley-Davidsons, to see them drinking and swaggering and staging drag races up the street. What was less wonderful,

particularly for other bikers, was when these gangs moved into dealing in bike thefts, a habit they have found hard to kick. Most bikers hate bike thieves and to have the thefts carried out on an organized basis by those who profess the biker lifestyle is hard to stomach. Even harder to stomach was when the Angels moved into drugs in a big way, not just using but dealing. The police slowly made some headway, but even now drug laboratories and distribution systems are found and broken up, all run by the Angels.

But bikes and strange substances often go hand in glove, and not just in the crazed imagination of Californian film producers. The film *Easy Rider*, which came out in 1969, wouldn't quite have been the same if Peter Fonda and

Top and left: Easy Rider was *the* cult bike film of the 1970s. First seen in 1969, it shocked or thrilled, depending on your viewpoint. Dennis Hopper and Peter Fonda (left with passenger Jack Nicholson) thundered their Panhead choppers right through the social mores of 1970. Sex 'n' drugs 'n' rock 'n' roll – and big bad Harleys – were inextricably linked. Note the amazing length of the forks and handlebars, the forward-mounted highway pegs and gallons of chrome on these hard-tailed muthas. *Above:* Californian Hells Angels have a social meet with the Crucifiers Los Angeles motorcycle club. Everyone rides a Harley to these tea-and-scone meets.

Dennis Hopper had got off their BMWs and downed a stiff lemonade. No, they had to have bad-ass Harleys, with ape-hanger bars, shabby bed-rolls, stars and stripes on the tank, stubble, shades, beer and drugs. It remains one of the greatest bike movies, although its ending must raise a few disturbing questions about red-neck tolerance.

All of the elements of speed, bikes, drugs, outlaws, beer and Harley-Davidsons come to life for real every March in Daytona, Florida. Cycle week is ostensibly all about the ultra-fast racing at the track, best summed up by an image of a few years ago: veteran hard man Kenny Roberts, flat on the tank of his Yamaha, a yellow and black screaming blur smearing round the banking at around 185 mph, slip-streaming other riders, passing within inches at maximum effort and speed until the very last second to haul the speed down to about 60 mph and Turn One. All the main racing factories are there, Honda, Yamaha and Suzuki, and some of the best riders in the world, but the grandstands are often half empty. Yet the town is full.

At one end of town is the beach, at the other the Speed-bowl. Moving between the two is a constant cavalcade of bikers who are put off by the screeching two-stroke racers and their space-age technology. Instead they want the re-assuring thump of a big four-stroke, they want to look mean and moody on their hogs, they want to get in a few beers and maybe watch a bit of racing. They are there for

Left: 'I wandered lonely as a cloud' on Daytona Beach, watched over only by the seagulls and traffic cops itching for a bust. *Above:* Bikers and their ol' ladies practice mean expressions before entering the Boot Hill Saloon, the Mecca for heavy drinking and heavy dudes during Cycle Week. The bikes outside range from early Electra Glides to current sportsters, but they're all Harleys. *Below:* Normally the two names are just separated by a hyphen, but Harley riders have a way with adjectives.

the show, yet they are part of the show themselves.

They cruise up and down Atlantic Avenue and Main Street, a black river of riders on their hogs, with bikes constantly joining the stream while others leave it to stick the bike on its sidestand and go for a beer. The Boot Hill Saloon is not the place for Gucci loafers or Lacoste casuals. You need grubby denims, stained by the miles and the weather – if nothing else – with heavy boots, a wallet on a chain, and a black T-shirt with suitable logo, like 'Harleys are best, fuck the rest', or 'My ol' lady yes, my dog maybe, my Harley-Davidson – Never'. And over this must come the sawn-off denim jacket with the patch on the back, displaying allegiance to the Angels, the Outlaws, the Fifth Chapter or whatever. Other useful street-cred additions are tattoos, beards, a beer belly and a slim ol' lady on the pillion, with her own denims, long hair and a T-shirt that she just loves raising to show off her tattoos.

If they read, this crowd will get *Easyriders* magazine, a basically Harleys-only mag that covers the world of the clubs, the girls, the contests and, of course, the bikes. There is now a sister magazine, *Foxyriders*, which is aimed solely at those women who occupy not the pillion but the

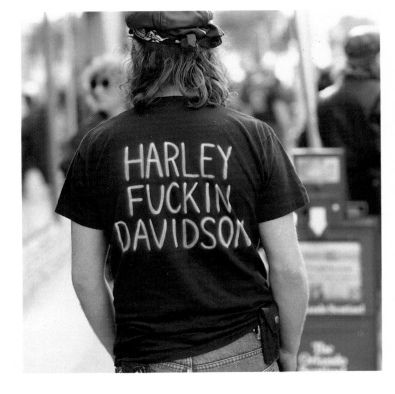

Above: Harley style takes all forms, but you just *know* he doesn't ride a Honda.
Right: A clean Tour Glide at Daytona reflects the sun off some custom paintwork. Only in America could those white-wall tyres stay so clean.

front seat of a Harley-Davidson.

The police tend to keep a high profile all week, busting anyone for anything remotely illegal, like speeding, getting drunk or taking any drugs, so it is largely safer being off the bike. Even riding down to the beach can be tricky, since you are only allowed to potter along the inviting yellow strip. The police pounce on anyone who tries to kick up a rooster of sand – riders stand the risk of being overtaken by joggers.

But back in town there is a constant flow of activity. One of the most famous events is the Rat's Hole Chopper Show on Boardwalk, where 'Big Daddy Rat' Smith runs a show for choppers, cruisers and vintage bikes. A man not much loved by feminists, his show draws some incredibly high-quality bikes from the surrounding states, many of them simply ridden there and stuck on their stands. Of course, if you aren't entering a Harley you don't stand a chance of winning.

The same goes for the whole week: if you aren't on a Harley you ain't shit. For some of the riders turning up on oriental bikes of incredible performance, dripping with advanced frame technology, race-replica braking systems and state-of-the-art ergonomics, all this seems a bit hard to fathom, as some middle-aged man goes by on his old Knucklehead, shaking and thumping along. What is even harder to take is his look: he's on a Harley and you're not and he pities you, you poor son-of-a-bitch.

The maligned rider of the foreign bike can take some comfort from the fact that all is not always what it seems. That middle aged man who looks like he spends all year on his bike cruising the country may well be a bank clerk

Left: All Harleys in the sunshine, from the 1930 WL 45 cu in at the front onwards. But this is not America, it is the Harley Super Rally of 1984, held at Brighton in England. *Above left:* Proud Englishman displays his 'colours' at the event. The beard, denim, shades, Harley and black helmet all show the US influence, but he is just too nice to be the real thing. Bad luck, old chap, nice try. *Above right:* Some advertising catches your eye more than others. A couple gaze out to sea, waiting for the tide to go out so that they can take their Harley onto the beach.

from Boston, who makes an annual pilgrimage down to Daytona. Along with all the chapters, the Angels, the Christian Bikers (God rides a Harley, remember?) comes a fair amount of showmanship, not to mention hypocrisy. Quite a few of the bikes that you see, even the big tourers, have not been ridden hundreds of miles just to be there: they have been trailered in on the back of vast Winnebago campers. They arrive in town, the owners change out of their shorts and check shirts and get into their scruffy bike gear and ride their Glides down Main Street a few times. At the end of the week they go back on the trailer and the biking threads get folded neatly away.

Of course, some of the dudes you see are for real, as is the menace in the air when two clubs clash, but Daytona Cycle Week remains a uniquely American dream product, and not all dreams are for real.

Elsewhere in the world, that American dream is largely represented by the Hells Angels on Harleys in virtually every European country as well as Australia. The Harley-Davidson Riders Club has national clubs that meet once a year for an international rally, with riders coming from Germany, Holland, Scandinavia and everywhere where they sell Harleys. Traditionally this has been the sort of

event where everyone meets in a muddy field, looks at the bikes, gets stone drunk on beer, tries a couple of competitions, then wanders off to throw up and fall over someone's tent. It is a traditional pastime, that has been much enjoyed by the more traditional rider for decades.

However, now is a period of transition. The Riders Club of Great Britain is in turmoil after the last international rally showed that not all riders want a Hells Angel riding through their tent in the middle of the night. The factory in Milwaukee may have the answer since they are launching the HOG groups abroad, so if you buy a new Harley you are automatically enroled in the national Owners Group. These groups have their own colours, and are run in chapters, which has given some countries, like Australia, some nervous moments since there is a clear correlation there between colours and Hells Angels. But these are strange times. In America, the backlash against the rebel image started by *The Wild One* back in the 1950s has been so successful that the HOG colours and chapters are now associated with families and charity outings. The Hells Angels, needless to say, want nothing to do with such a clean image and stay well clear. The rebel image has gone full circle.

4

CUSTOM

IF YOU WANT A HARLEY-DAVIDSON IT IS UNDERSTOOD THAT YOU DON'T WANT A CAR OR BIKE LIKE THE

AVERAGE JOE; YOU NEED TO BE DIFFERENT. ONCE YOU HAVE ONE IT IS EQUALLY ESSENTIAL THAT IT DOESN'T

LOOK EXACTLY LIKE ANYONE ELSE'S, SINCE THAT WOULD MAKE YOU LIKE THEM. HOW DIFFERENT YOU DECIDE

TO BE, AND HOW THAT DESIRE IS EXPRESSED IN THE BIKE, IS WHAT MAKES THEM SUCH ART FORMS ON WHEELS,

AND WHAT MAKES THEM SUCH PSYCHOLOGICAL STATEMENTS OF SELF ■

Custom work ranges from tanks *(left)* to whole machines *(above)*. This Shovelhead, photographed in Brighton, England, has custom hardtail frame, and tricked out motor and cycle parts. But it's not to the highest standard — not the crude engraving on the rear brake torque arm, and a clear change of mind between spraying front and rear wheels.

For as long as people have been making bikes, other people have been changing them to suit their requirements, even if the main requirement is simply to be different. Ever since they were launched Harleys have been open to the same market pressures but, to their credit, they seem to have reacted to styling changes, if not to demands for advanced engineering, faster than many other manufacturers. The main time of change came in the 1960s, when the rebel and would-be renegade wanted something that set him apart from the straights.

The result was the chopper, a disaster in engineering terms. As the front forks grew and grew like some giant bean-stalk, their ability to actually make the front wheel go up and down diminished, while the standard rake and trail dictates went out the window, along with weight distribution. However, for a long highway a long wheelbase gave a lot of stability, while the forward-mounted foot-pegs, high bars and rear cissy bars let the rider sit back and while the miles away. Needless to say, *Easy Rider* in 1969 was a catalyst in chopper growth, and soon everyone

wanted one, although the standard of workmanship varied from the lovely to the lethal.

One man who led the trend in terms of artistic imagination and metal skills was Arlen Ness, a quiet Californian whose first bike was a Knucklehead. He soon started to subtly alter it, and then started getting commis-

sions to do the same to others' bikes. He basically invented the Low Rider, which started out as the Bay Area Low Rider, correctly deducing that simply sticking on long forks could be dangerous. He lowered the cycle all round, then changed the lines to a sway-back grace, then stripped everything unnecessary off like fairings, fat seat and mud-

Variations on a theme. A classic and clean chopper, *main pic*, displays over-length forks with truly minimal suspension. *Inset:* This custom is more influenced by the Low Rider style pioneered by Arlen Ness, with low, lean lines and classy engraving. It's got decent suspension, too.

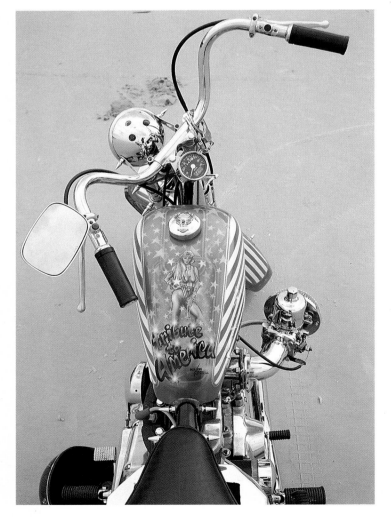

guards, then added engraving and some brilliantly exe-cuted paintwork, chrome and gold. Somehow he man-aged to make the whole device look tasteful as well as fast and, most importantly, different.

Since then Harley themselves have copied the Low Rider theme, although most H-D dealerships in America also sell Arlen Ness products. Within the factory Willie G. Davidson realized back about the time of *Easy Rider* that riders were not content to have the two ranges, sports and touring, with nothing much in between. It was his idea not to make a totally new bike, at a cost of millions of dol-lars as the Japanese would do, but to see what could be done with what already existed. It is an attitude that has always been something of a trademark with the factory, which is good because it keeps development costs down, and bad because always turning inwards isn't necessarily the best way to go forward. But in this case Davidson moved rapidly forward.

Putting the Sportsters XL forks on to the FL motor and

Top: A custom Super Glide; *left:* custom carb well out in the breeze; *right:* painting, plating and engraving; *far right:* massively over-length forks on a chopper – all are examples of the way individual owners feel they have to change their standard machines. As a result they don't get away to freedom and individuality, they simply get re-classified: Low Rider, Chopper, trad, retro.

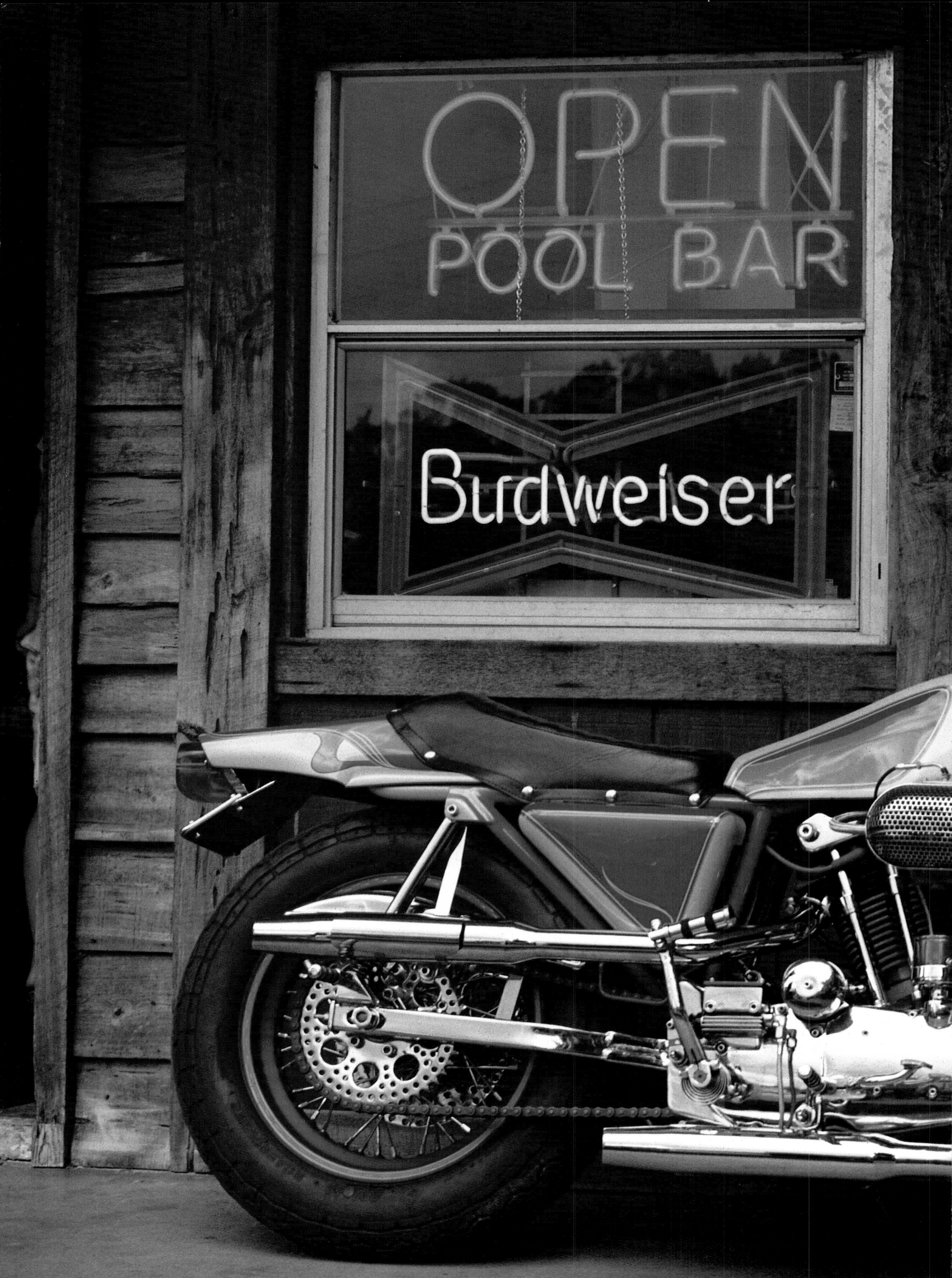
OPEN
POOL BAR
Budweiser

Left: An unusually European-looking custom, a 1977 XLCH. This 1000 cc Sportster would look equally at home in Europe or America. *Inset:* Artwork is often of exceptionally high standard: this tank shows a screamin' eagle over a Harley canyon racing — actually a form of racing not really suited to the majority of slow-handling Harleys.

Top left: Work never stops at Daytona. Pinstriping by night on a Low Rider. *Left:* A 1970 Sportster displaying deep-throat carb, gold-plating and neat engraving. Pity they forgot the underside of the gas tank. *Above:* Beauty is in the eye of the beholder, but even the owner has to wear shades to look at it. Somewhere under there is an Electra Glide, but on top of it 1400 lamps. Snapped at the Rat's Hole Show, Daytona, this mobile Las Vegas displays the ethic of 'Too much is just enough'.

chassis instantly lightened the whole bike, improving handling and looks. The Super Glides was really the first cruiser, and also one of the first factory customs. It led on to a whole host of bikes like the Wide Glide and the Fat Boy, although at the time many wondered whether it was wise for the factory to customize bikes themselves; after all, if it came from the factory it couldn't be a custom, could it? The Super Glide made that question hard to answer. Since then, even though the number of new power plants has been minimal, the number of options that you can have make it easy to get a hog slightly different to anyone else's, which is the name of the game.

Since the 1970s the chopper has faded slowly, in part because it simply can't pass more stringent traffic regulations, but also because it was a fashion, and all fashions pass. The look now is to go even further backwards, with bikes like Harley's FLST Heritage Softail, which has the bulbous, opulent lines of the hard-tail 1949 Hydra Glide, but with rear suspension cunningly built into the design under the seat. Such is progress: two forward, one back then two forward.

Such bikes as the Softail show up the fact that, although several framers sell genuine hard-tail frames for H-Ds, most people now want some comfort in their biking. None more so than the tourers. Their modifications have often simply been additions rather than changes. Big 1340cc Harleys can take several hundred pounds of lug-

gage but even so some of them seem strained to the limit with panniers and top-boxes as big as tea chests, fairings with the frontage of a Peterbilt truck and enough lights to drain a power station. Taste is an individual quality, and in America it comes right out in the open, from the understated lean lines of a Ness Low Rider to the full dresser Wurlitzer on wheels of an Electra Glide with the works, including filligreed and chased metalwork over every surface, and banks of lights all over the rear.

The whole point of customizing is to stamp your own personality on a product that comes out of a factory, even if that product has a whole heap of personality to start with. But in California there now comes a company that is playing this game the other way round. Cycle Boyz creates its own customs, its own wacky ideas in metal, and then finds buyers who decide that this is the extension of their particular personality. You would have to be a certain sort of person to have such a public statement made about your personality by someone else, but hey, this is the West Coast. Zebra stripes, replica-ish 1950s police bikes or a sort of pre-war Knucklehead using the Evolution motor are just some of the results of Cycle Boyz' manic creativity. Prices are strictly Hollywood, with bikes starting at $25,000 and rising to not far off $50,000. But the bikes will sell, boss Carl Jones claims, 'because anything with the name Harley-Davidson on it sells like you won't believe.'

STARDOM

HARLEYS ARE STARS IN THEIR OWN RIGHT, AND HAVE HAD THE LEAD ROLE IN AT LEAST ONE MAJOR MOVIE.

BUT THEIR SADDLES HAVE HELD SOME EQUALLY FAMOUS BEHINDS, FROM KINGS TO POLITICIANS, FROM

ACTORS TO BOXERS. H-DS HAVE BEEN RIDDEN BY MUHAMMAD ALI, OLIVIA NEWTON-JOHN, CROWN PRINCE

OLAF OF NORWAY, NEIL DIAMOND AND CLINT EASTWOOD, AND THE WHOLE WORLD CAST OF ANYONE WHO

IS SOMEONE. UNLESS YOU'RE A NOBODY YOU'VE GOT TO HAVE ONE ■

Left: The gas tank says it all. *Above:* Liz Taylor and her 883 Sportster with arch capitalist Malcolm
Forbes and the Capitalist Tools in the background.

Anyone who buys a Harley-Davidson feels a bit special, and it's easy to feel something of a star if you ride around on a really trick Harley. But what if someone who is already a star wants to ride a Harley? The two actually seem to go together really well, a partnership rather than a master-servant relationship. After all, Harleys have even had films made about them, whereas the actors just appear in them.

The 1973 film *Electra Glide in Blue* is the only film to be named after a motorbike. It wasn't about outlaw bike gangs but about a highway patrolman and his obsession with the title of the film. To European viewers, riding lean Triumphs or fat'n'fast Z1 Kawasakis, his dream bike seemed obese and over-dressed, like he was lusting after an overweight aunt, but his feelings for the bike hit the nerve even if they seemed misplaced. At least the thing was stable: when he gets blown off it at the end it seems to ride on by itself for ever – a sequence probably sponsored by Harley-Davidson.

Another antidote to the 'only outlaws ride bikes' mentality was the film *On Any Sunday,* which was basic-ally a documentary of motorbike competition, based around a season with H-D's top factory rider, Bert Law-will. It helped the audience understand what biking and racing were all about, and of course did Bert's career no harm whatsoever.

Bikes offer welcome anonymity to any well-known face, since a full-face helmet and tinted visor hides even the best-known features. This defence is rather wasted if the rider then doesn't wear a crash helmet. In California, where a helmet is not a legal requirement, at least for now, the roads are full of the rich and famous posing around on bikes. However, a recent spate of crashes involving actors

Stars from around the world. *Top left:* Robert Blake, star of *Electra Glide in Blue,* dreaming of his fantasy bike. *Top right:* Steve Jones of the 'Sex Pistols' on an FLH. *Opposite top right:* Ringo Starr and Barbara Bach on an Electra Glide. *Opposite top left:* Terence Trent d'Arby on modified Heritage Softail Classic. *Main pic:* Michael Hutchence of Australia's rock group INXS on a Hydra Glide.

like James Caan, might well put them back under fibre-glass and plastic.

Some of the top people like the pose of a Japanese bike, a technological fighter plane image, but plenty more like to buy American and buy Harley. Hogs have always been popular with the stars, even back before the last world war. During the war plenty of actors rode around on their Harleys, including Clark Gable, who owned a 1942 EL. Instead of a helmet he usually wore a hat and a sardonic smile.

Quite a few only rode bikes for publicity purposes, people like Marlene Dietrich, Jimmy Durante and Tyrone Power, but plenty more rode them for real. Elvis Presley loved Harleys almost as much as meat-loaf, and owned several including a KH. To enjoy a Harley you could be an actor, like Roy Rogers, Burt Reynolds and Steve McQueen, or a singer, like Bob Dylan, Cher and Lou Reed, or simply somebody, like Sir Malcolm Campbell, Charles Lindbergh and Arnold Schwarzenegger.

One somebody who had a long relationship with the H-D factory was stunt-man Robert 'Evel' Knievel. After a series of bone-crushing but spectacular stunts, Knievel was given a certain amount of backing by the factory along with several XR-based bikes. The deal was good for Knievel but it was also good for the factory, since it gained an incredible amount of publicity, never mind that their product was usually seen upside down or flying into a parked bus. The sequence where he tries to leap the fountain at Caesar's Palace in Las Vegas but lands awkwardly and crashes in grisly, bone-shattering slow motion, must be one of the most repeated clips of film

next to man landing rather more successfully on the Moon. The relationship foundered in 1974, after Knievel's Flash Gordon rocket failed to do anything except sink gracelessly into the Snake River Canyon.

Most actors, of course, never attempt any dangerous stunts, even if the part demands it. Stunt-men make a lucrative living out of doing all the dangerous bits, for which the actor gets the credit. English stunt-man Jim Dowdall has doubled for most of them in films from *Where Eagles Dare* to *Superman*, and along the way picked

up a love of Harleys, not to mention picking up quite a few rare Harleys as well – after getting blown off a WLA in a battle sequence you develop a certain feeling for it. Recent additions include several from Steve McQueen's collection, which was broken up on his death. Jim got the bikes because of a long friendship with Bud Ekins, who provided most of the Harleys for war films and oversaw Steve McQueen's extensive collection of bikes. It is Ekins who actually jumps the barbed wire in *The Great Escape*.

Above: English stuntman Jim Dowdall with Steve McQueen's red 1936 1400 cc flat head. To the left is a Second World War BMW combo, to the right is a 1957 Hydra Glide. The following year this model got rear suspension to become the Duo Glide. Harriet the Harris Hawk acts as a devastatingly effective security system. *Top right:* Steve McQueen (actually Bud Ekins) on a Triumph does 'That Jump' in *The Great Escape*. *Far Left:* The most famous stunt man of all, Evel Knievel, readies himself for a leap into hospital aboard a modified XR750.

Left: Sylvester Stallone sneers aboard a not-quite-stock Harley outside the 'Johnny Rocket' restaurant in LA. *Above left:* Billy Idol's sneer doesn't work quite so well. *Above:* Malcolm Forbes on his Heritage Softail in front of holiday home. *Top:* Peter de Savary, who owns Littlecote, the scene of the first rally for the English Harley Owners Group. Seen here aboard an Ultra Classic, he claims he frightened himself so much on the open road that he bought one for London and one for the country — and drove or flew between the two.

The current rise in H-D popularity has been mirrored in the number of actors and other stars who now own Harleys. The bikes seem to instantly strike a chord with the owner. Actor Patrick Swayze was asked if he would give up biking – their agents and insurance companies loathe actors riding the contraptions. 'No', he replied, 'not my Harley. That's my love.' Actor Mickey Rourke thought about his bike: 'Harley? It's a personal thing, that can't be described.' Sylvester Stallone also rides Harleys, although he doesn't talk about them much.

One man who can hardly be called inarticulate is Malcolm Forbes, one of the richest men in the world thanks to *Forbes* magazine, with a fortune worth over six hundred million dollars. A gregarious *bon viveur,* Forbes likes nothing better than roaming the world on semi-diplomatic goodwill tours. He always rides a Harley, as do his self-styled 'Capitalistic Tools' followers. Poor parts of the planet have been stunned by the arrival of the Forbes entourage, with outriders, trucks, press, and a huge cavalcade of Harleys thundering through some dusty hamlet.

SPEED

FROM THE 1920S WRECKING CREW TO THE 1980S 'LUCIFER'S HAMMER', HARLEY-DAVIDSONS HAVE BEEN

WINNING RACES ON EVERY KIND OF SURFACE, FROM TARMAC TO DIRT. HARLEYS HAVE TRAVELLED AT OVER

250MPH, WHILE TWIN-ENGINED DRAGSTERS HAVE DEAFENED SPECTATORS AROUND THE WORLD. EVEN IN AN

AGE OF JAPANESE PERFORMANCE SUPREMACY, HARLEYS CAN STILL CUT IT ON THE ROUGH WITHOUT TAKING

RECOURSE TO THE TACTICS OF EARLIER DECADES, WHEN THE MOTTO WAS SOMETIMES 'IF AT FIRST YOU DON'T

SUCCEED, CHANGE THE RULES' ■

Left: Harley hero Jay Springsteen high on the hog at a US TT race. Springsteen won every race on every type of Harley from the XR750 here to a road racing XR1000. *Above:* Marion Owens on 3700 cc of double-engined Harley power at the drag strip.

Speed is something traditionally associated with any motorbike, but it must be said that Harleys have not always lived up to that reputation. The accepted parameters of what is fast were blown to pieces by the arrival of the high-revving, multi-cylinder, multi-valve, double overhead-cam Japanese sports bikes. A Sportster may have a more than satisfactory amount of animal grunt, but it would be torquing to itself if fronted against a Yamaha Genesis or Kawasaki ZX10, or a host of bikes with only half the capacity. It must be remembered that H-D didn't have a production five-speed gearbox until 1980, and that the Sportster's gearbox still has numerous parts bearing 1958 stamps. The latest accessories catalogue is 80 pages long, packed with bits that you can add to your Harley. Only about half a dozen of those pages cover the Screamin' Eagle performance parts.

Having said that, you can make a Harley-Davidson go very fast indeed. The World Speed Record for a single-engined motorbike is still held by H-D. On 16 October 1970 racer Cal Rayborn ran a Sportster-based Streamliner across the salt flats at 265.42mph. His exploits appear in *On Any Sunday,* where he can be seen discovering that the bike steered normally up to about 150mph, needed to be 'steered the other way' from 150-200mph and then back to normal from then on. He discovered this by trial and terror, crashing several times but finally clinching the record that stood until 1985. That year Dan Kinsey rode another streamliner, 'Tenacious', to a speed of 276.51mph, a new

Above: Joe Petrali on his record-breaking Knucklehead. In 1937, on his 61 cu in ohv Twin, Petrali set a new record of 137.183 mph at Daytona Beach.

record that still stands.

In truth, the factory has had a rather inconsistent attitude towards competition, some years putting together proper teams, other years letting the whole thing drain away. At one time or another Harleys have been used for just about every form of racing, like hillclimbs, drag racing, off-road, road racing and flat track. Racing bikes include a twin-cam eight-valver not from this decade but from 1916, when the famous Wrecking Crew gunned the 61 cu in twins to numerous victories.

In the 1920s Harley technology really got going, with twin cams, eight valves, two exhaust ports per cylinder,

Above: An immaculate 1919 61 cu in Twin, built and rebuilt for go as well as show.

A lovely little 1927 single-cylinder speedway racer. These singles came in four versions, from side-valve to overhead valve generator model. Joe Petrali was destroying the opposition on his little 'peashooter' as late as 1935.

decent drum brakes and three-speed gearboxes all appearing on various racing bikes, like the early superbike 1928 JDH two-cam. But the period in the 1930s belonged not to a bike but to a man, Joe Petrali. As early as 1925 Petrali broke the 100mph barrier in a board race, and throughout the 1930s he simply destroyed anyone who challenged him on road, board or hillclimb. His incredible successes helped the factory through a lean time as they discovered that racing really does rub off on the marque – something they have seemed to forget from time to time since then.

Although they were not exactly hogs, the Aermacchi two-stroke 250cc and 350cc twins, born out of the buyout in 1960, did bring H-D racing wins. In the hands of Walter Villa, the twins took the 250cc World Championship from 1974 to 1976 and then the 350cc the following year. But to many people such bikes were not Harleys – what they wanted were thundering four-strokes.

They wanted the regime of what had gone before, with bikes like the 767cc KR racers of the 1950s and 1960s which won a dozen National titles for the factory against some fierce opposition, which is remarkable for a side-valve engine. It would have been even more remarkable if the factory and the racing committee hadn't conspired to keep things going H-D's way. The threat came from the sweet-handling Triumphs, Nortons and other British bikes, which could easily out-manoeuvre the clumsier Harleys. First the rules changed to enable the KR's lower compression ratio to form a new rule and then, when that failed, it was ruled that the 750 side-valve should only race

A later XR750 – but it isn't. In 1987 Harley-Davidson bought Armstrong Equipment's manufacturing rights for the MT500 military cycle. This Harley has the Armstrong engine, actually a Rotax single, but with new Harley crankcase covers.

The KR was not one of Harley's better bikes. The side-valve 750 cc Twin needed reboring after the first 200 miles because of cylinder distortion and it got worse from there.

Gene Church, who won the Battle of the Twins championship three years running on 'Lucifer's Hammer'.

against 500cc overhead valved bikes. This let Cal Rayborn and the KR romp away with the title until 1969 when the rules became slightly more even-handed.

The KR's replacement, the XR750, needed no rules in its favour for a while. It was a splendid bike, a bike that still casts a long shadow over flat track racing and has formed the basis for many factory racers, both road and dirt, as well as enabling Evel Knievel to catapult himself to fame and injury. Cal Rayborn won numerous road races on a modified XR, but failed to really get to grips with the dirt-bike version, although plenty of other riders had no problems. The XR750 led to the XR1000, which in turn led to successes in the fledgling Battle of the Twins series, a series just for two-cylinder four-strokes.

In its first year, 1983, the XR1000 won the BoTT at Daytona piloted by the dirt-track expert Jay Springsteen, clocking 167mph on the way. Springer, under Dick O'Brien, consistently won on Harleys, on every type of surface from short-track to mile dirt tracks to Daytona road races on everything from an Aermacchi to the XR1000. His success in Battle of the Twins, realistically the only road race series where Harleys stood a chance of winning, was followed up by another Harley rider, Gene Church. He dominated the series for three years, winning the championship from 1984–86 on the mighty 'Lucifer's Hammer', a bike sponsored by the Harley Owners Group. Since then things have gone to Honda.

Erik Buell, an ex-employee of the company, decided that a proper racing bike was the way to go, at a time when the factory obviously didn't. He left the company and set up on his own to produce a remarkably Bimota-like racer, that Gene Church rode for the 1987 season: 'Lucifer's Hammer II'. It handled sweetly and looked dramatic, if rather bulbous, and its iron XR1000 engine put out around 112bhp for the race track. He also made a road version of the racer, although whether Americans were ready for something that was a Harley but looked so radical is open

to question. A further question mark is, if they were ready, did they want a new chassis with the old engine rather than the new Evolution motor? But in many ways the Buell bikes are the sharp-handling Harleys that the factory should have produced.

In flat track racing Harley have again run up against the might and resources of the Honda factory, as well as the incredible talent of Honda's number one rider, Bubba Shobert. However, while racing in the 500cc World Championship road races in 1989, Bubba was seriously injured, leaving the way for the coveted AMA No 1 plate to return to Harley-Davidson thanks to the skilful riding of Jay Springsteen's ex-team mate Scott Parker.

Drag racing has always been a popular Harley pastime. It really got into gear after the Second World War, when numerous disgruntled ex-GIs started thrashing their hogs down main streets, across salt lakes and anywhere else where there was a clean quarter. By 1970 single-engined

The dirt-track racer of the 1970s was the XR750 – note the lack of any front brakes. With riders like Jay Springsteen, XRs won just about every race for a decade. It is still a considerable force in US dirt-track racing, and wins without cheating.

Erik Buell builds the sort of Italian-inspired frames that the factory should have done for their Sportsters. This pearlescent RR1200 is owned by 1988 CART champion Danny Sullivan.

Harleys were already getting below the nine-second quarter barrier with terminals of over 150mph. The subsequent twin-engined monsters, some burning nitro, upped the stakes again, with Marion Owen upholding Harley-Davidson honour throughout the late 1970s. Drag racing is something that a lot of owners associate with, since tarmac racing is not really their league or their scene. Everyone from outlaws to suppressed middle aged execs likes to let rip on the strip, and 'run what you brung' meets retain popularity at a time when the top drag bikes bear absolutely no resemblance to anything you could ride on the road for more than a few seconds.

The factory has had a rather ambivalent attitude towards racing, particularly road racing, throughout its history. Current chairman Vaughn Beals has said that he is not very interested in a racing programme, at a time when the company can sell every bike it produces without the horrific expense and effort of a full race programme. On the other hand, some elements within the company feel that racing success has served them well in the past and could do so in the future. Persistent rumours of a new racing engine plus the odd little piece of information indicates that a new V-twin racing engine may well appear soon and, if it does, it will have at least four, possibly five valves, with DOHC, fuel injection and all the other gizzmos one normally associates with the Japanese bikes. America has the riding talent, all it lacks is a competitive home-grown product. This could be it.

DRESSING

HOG-HEAVEN TO SOME PEOPLE IS AN ELECTRA GLIDE COVERED IN BANKS OF FLASHING LIGHTS GLINTING OFF

MILES OF CHROME. TO OTHERS AESTHETIC PERFECTION IS A PINK SADDLE, MATCHING LEATHERS AND AIR-

BRUSHED MURALS OF CONAN THE LIBRARIAN. THE WORLD OF HARLEY-DAVIDSON IS A WORLD OF SELF-

EXPRESSION IN METAL AND, OF COURSE, IN CLOTHES. DRESS YOUR HOG, DRESS YOURSELF, GET OUT ON THE

ROAD AND CRUISE FOR EVER ■

Electra Glides in various hues. Trying to stand out in a crowd like this drives owners to greater and
greater excess.

If you won a Honda or a Kawasaki or whatever, you can usually buy a set of leathers to match the bike or the current GP star, and perhaps a sweatshirt and T-shirt but that is about all. If you own a Harley you can choose your accessories from a 40-page catalogue. The amazing thing about Harley accessories is not just their volume, but their width of choice. Who else but Harley-Davidson would offer extremely tasteful gold jewellery, trench coats, watches, women's underwear and handbags?

Theoretically, you could dress in H-D clothing from the moment you got up in the morning to the moment you went back to bed, in between taking in a bike ride, a business meeting and a romantic dinner for two. Some of the stuff is a bit country and western, a bit fringed and flounced for some tastes, but other gear, some of it designed by Willie G. himself, would pass muster in any restaurant or race paddock in the world. The leathers are all of good, soft quality and make excellent riding gear, although riding chaps are perhaps best worn by Americans rather than London poseurs, who might given the tight black leather brigade the wrong idea.

Once you are fully kitted out you can consider what else the company has to offer. The list of extras includes such items as tankards, trucks, clocks, lighters, beach towels and even a collector's curio cabinet to put everything in. The point as far as the factory is concerned is not only to

On-board radios and cassettes are fairly common now, but this early Pioneer radio on an early Electra Glide must have been really cool. The chrome helps reception.

Warr's shop in Chelsea, England, is typical Harley back to the future. Old engines, posters, and paraphernalia remind the potential buyer of earlier decades of history, legend and image. All of which helps when it comes to paying modern prices.

The combination of fluffy pink and a Nazi helmet is one of the least bizarre things about this bike. With these Wurlitzer-on-wheels customs, it's not just the obvious things that make you either point or gag, it's the details, like the little hinged covers over the end of the exhausts.

make a lot of money out of all these accessories, but to keep Harley-Davidson on your mind, part of your life whether you are on the bike or off it. Europe's oldest Harley dealer, F. H. Warr & Sons Ltd in the King's Road, London, has been running since 1924, selling Harleys exclusively since 1953, and perfectly sums up the Harley attitude. The shop is not full of bits of old exhaust systems and cheap jackets slung in a heap, but has mahogany cabinets, a Wurlitzer and a pretty full range of clothing from leather jackets and jeans to camisoles, nighties and chaps (a devastating combination). It also sells motorcycles and spares. You are surrounded by the Harley logo and name so you can't forget for a second that this is not a bike shop, this is a Harley-Davidson shop.

The company is very hot on safeguarding its logos and spends a considerable amount of effort in nailing dealers and traders who use any H-D trademark without authorization. The list of H-D trademarks extends far beyond just the Harley-Davidson bar and shield and includes Fat Bob, Sturgis, Screamin' Eagle and Wide Glide as well as some you wouldn't expect, like More Than A Machine and By The People, For The People.

Of course, if you really like Harleys you wouldn't consider for a second getting all dressed up yourself while leaving the bike looking less than properly dressed. Most owners of Japanese bikes improve their bikes by taking things off them – unless adding a turbo – but Harley-Davidson owners normally do the opposite. A lot of

'Boss Hog II' is almost classy by comparison. A small battery of lights, reflectors and chrome goo-gaws livens up the otherwise relatively plain rear end.

You don't have to be young to ride a Harley. When you pick one out like this it's as comfortable as your Cadillac, although perhaps not quite as snug as the one at the top of the previous page. This Harley has been customized using not just Harley accessories. The Vetter fairing should keep the flies off the pink trouser suit, but don't forget the matching lipstick, and pray you don't get an oil leak.

accessories for Harleys don't even pretend to do anything useful like making the bike go faster or handle better. Instead they are there to add glitter to your Glide, with chrome engine covers, light strips that run right round top boxes and panniers, chrome axle nuts, chrome extender caps for the exhaust pipes and more chrome everything. Then there are even more comfortable seats for the tourers, which can come complete with real sheepskin covers (it is not recommended that you get into the saddle after a rainstorm), screens to keep the bugs out of your teeth since Harley riders wear open-face helmets, and racks. Tour-Pak top boxes and panniers to give you the carrying capacity for at least six Mexicans.

All of this is to try and instil into the buyer that owning a Harley-Davidson is a way of life. In the past this has been a relatively easy exercise since the average buyer was happy to accept the latest Yank Tank from the factory without too much criticism. Now, with the market splitting into numerous groups, each of which has to be satisfied, the job is more difficult. A good ol' boy from Texas may well feel that buying a Tour Glide will take him straight to hog heaven, but a lawyer in New York is going to take some persuading that a bike that vibrates, has poor ergonomics, may well leak oil and is not particularly fast is the bike for him instead of a 170mph oriental missile that reflects tech-

nological progress from every streamlined surface.

The sales figures show that Harley-Davidson are winning the battle, although it is too early to say if they will win the war. To do this they have shown that owning a Harley is not a static relationship but a developing one. If you own a Honda Aspencade there really isn't very much you can add to it, either in the way of factory accessories or as after-market goodies, whereas a Harley can be changed to reflect the sort of owner you are. Your personality can also be further aired by choosing the right gear, either from the Harley catalogue, or from the huge market that caters for all the types of bike rider. You can present to the world an image that you feel exactly represents your character – or the character you would like to have. And that image, your personality, is catered for by the factory of Harley-Davidson, who will look after every facet, who have a product for every aspect of your life from boots to helmet, from huge fender to chromed and hooded tail-light, from the mug you drink to your child's T-shirt.

Some of the things you can buy either for yourself or for your hog would simply appal a European owner but to really get the most out a Harley-Davidson, whether you are a Born-Again Biker, an RUB – Rich Urban Biker – or a Hells Angel, to really understand and appreciate it, you have to be one thing: American.

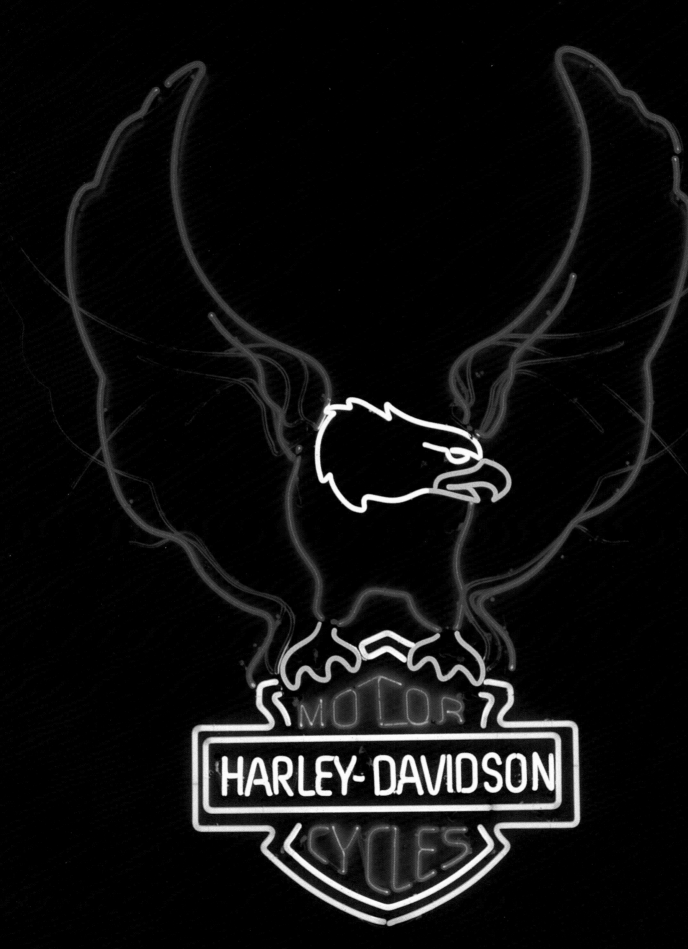

INDEX